WASHED IN THE WATER

TALES FROM THE SOUTH

by Nancy Hartney

Nancy Hartney
November 2013

Washed in the Water: Tales from the South
Copyright © 2013 Nancy Hartney
All rights reserved

Published by
Pen-L Publishing
12 West Dickson #4455
Fayetteville, AR 72702

First Edition
ISBN: 978-0-9851274-5-9

Illustrations by Susan Raymond
Cover and interior design by Kimberly Pennell
Printed and bound in USA

More books at Pen-L.com.

WASHED

IN THE

WATER

TALES
FROM
THE
SOUTH

By Nancy Hartney

For my mother, Mildred Almand Davis,
and
Robert J. Hartney, my own sweet man.

Table of Contents

Washed in the Water 1

The Day the Snake Got Killed 23

The Cane Grinding 35

The Fig Trees 55

More Than Fruitcake 71

Last Love 87

The Stooper 107

Washed in the Water

~~~~~~

Lisa Dell thought about rivers a lot. People, too. She found it hard to say exactly where things began and where they ended.

Take the Suwannee River. Blackwater spilled out of the Okefenokee Swamp, flowed through scrub and palmetto-choked land, and ended up in the Gulf of Mexico. Moss-draped branches dabbled sweeper fingers in the current most of the way.

Likewise, a church community filled up with folks and flowed in swirls and eddies through shadows and sunshine. God's True Word Baptist Church near Ellaville seemed to do that. Most ever' September, the congregation put on a tent meeting to revive and re-awaken their Christian faith and draw in new members. Folks living out in pinelands came into town and camped under great oaks for an entire week, sometimes longer. Locals came early of a morning and stayed into evening. Preaching, singing, jawing and general neighboring went on all day and into late night hours.

Lisa Dell's mother, a pinched, nervous woman, insisted Lisa come to take care of other folks' children, sing in the choir, and help with cooking for revival week. In other words, to work.

After six children, her Daddy got worn out and run off. Mama sent the younger brothers and sisters to live with relatives. Two oldest boys drifted off and never looked back. Shed of everyone but Lisa Dell, Mama proceeded to push her into day cleaning with white town folks that didn't want coloreds. Lisa didn't mind the work, but she hated for Mama to take *all* her folding money and any hand-me-down clothes she brought home. And she hated enduring the perspiring clutches of an employer driving her back to their rent house after a day's drudgery. Lisa was Mama's only ticket and Lisa resented that.

Although heavy set, Lisa was still a striking girl-woman with her raven hair, olive complexion and acorn-brown eyes. She lacked self-confidence though and often chewed her nails down to the quick, leaving raw, ragged hangnails outlining each finger.

Her mother berated her shy ways, admonishing her to throw herself into the spirit of love at the camp meetings, enjoy the touch of others, and, especially, to seek out the minister. Lisa chafed at her mother's manipulations. She made excuses by saying she had to finish breakfast or dinner, take care of the children, or practice choir.

On the last night of the autumn gathering, Lisa sat outside and watched kids while they slept on quilts under the trees. Mosquitoes buzzed incessantly and caused one or another of the children to stir and scratch at bites.

Sweat trickled between her breasts and hair kinked into wet, wispy ringlets around her face. She sat outside listening as gospel singing shook the church house panes and folks raised their voices in a great musical petition. Surely a better life awaited in the hereafter. Of all things religious, Lisa loved singing best. Usually she sang in choir or did solos. Folks said God smiled at her rich alto voice.

Oil-soaked rag torches lit the entrance to the

church grounds, throwing shadows across the lichen-covered stone wall. She watched men and boys drift out to stand under ancient oaks and visit over a jug. She noticed couples, some married, some not, slip away into the graveyard to lay behind a family marker. Maybe, like her, they felt safer among the departed.

For the last hour, she had sat against a tree and moved the hot air around with a hand fan advertising Moore Brothers Insurance. She got precious little relief from it.

Lisa Dell always thought Jesus Christ a radical who walked in the dust with the unloved, un-valued, and dispossessed. He talked against govern-ment and berated religions of the day. They got Him for it too. Tried, convicted, and sentenced to die – all quite legally.

In her heart she knew Preacher Westerly, an itinerant self-taught minister, railed against her ideas as blasphemous. She also knew him to tip the bottle. When he was into the devil's brew, his lecherous nature rose up and took over.

During the Friday evening call to salvation, her mother had shoved her forward in front of the entire congregation. She had knelt at the flimsy wood rail and taken Christ as her personal savior in a thin whisper.

The Sabbath crowned revival week when Lisa Dell knew she and other born again petitioners would be baptized in the Suwannee.

Nagging questions played in her mind: *Am I getting washed in the water for me 'cause I gotta respect what Jesus did? Or am I doing it in answer to my sweet granny's dying wish? Mama pushed me into this in front of the whole church so maybe it's to save face for her? Could water really wash away sin? How much do I have to believe?*

On the other hand, seemed like everybody expected it after spending four days living with and among them. Especially Preacher. He had panted after her the entire time. Easiest thing to do, just be quiet and get baptized.

When final service ended, folks ambled out to catch an evening breath of air, gather up sleeping children, and saunter off to their camps. She helped the last of them, and then stood under ancient oaks, dreamily watching fireflies. Breezes, balanced somewhere between oven-hot and summer-sodden, slowly stirred.

Preacher sidled up right behind her. A sour

stink forewarned her even before she felt his dry, scruffy fingers.

"Get your gnarly old hands off me. You supposed to be a man of the cloth. You supposed to stay away from drink. You supposed to set an example." She edged further around the tree.

"Sister Lisa Dell, you a woman that God made ample. He done that meaning for you to share yourself." Stumping his toe on a protruding root, Preacher fell to one knee. Bracing himself against the sticky bark of a pine, he wobbled upright and, undeterred, inched around the tree licking his lips.

"Your mother is a good woman." He staggered slightly, slurring his words, as he attempted to whisper in her ear. "You done accepted our Savior during the call. You gonna be gettin' baptized on Sunday morning."

"I know that. Mama made me go up to that altar."

"Let's go over yonder under them other trees. We can pray together and I can guide you." Swaying, Preacher reached for her.

"No." Lisa backed up a step, wringing her hands. "I think we can talk over by that torch near yonder gate." She pointed toward the church yard entrance. "Over there. In the light."

"No, Sister, no. You come with me over under them fur oaks." He gestured to a dark pool of shadow. "My truck's there. We can sit so's I can guide you. Private like." He snatched at her, stumbled, and fell face down into pine straw. Drooling, he rose to his knees and motioned toward her. "Come git me up. I cain't make it on my own."

Tentative, she extended her hand. Rabid dog-like, he grabbed her wrist and held it in a vise grip. She braced against him as he pulled himself upright.

"Your mother done told me to *be* with you." He grunted, spewing a sour fog inches from her face.

Uncertain, she jerked her head away. Her hair whipped across his face as she turned.

"You smell. In fact, you stink. Mama does mean things to me, but I ain't going with you."

"Don't rise up against your mother and against the Lord. He commanded children to honor they parents. You do as you been told." Glaring, he yanked her step-by-step across the hard-pack yard toward the dark fringe of pines and his dented pickup.

"God meant you to share yourself. You a handmaiden just like Biblical Hagar and are saved forever." He fumbled a moment, breathing hard, and then stumbled on. He pulled her with him.

At the truck, Preacher shoved Lisa Dell against a rusty wheel well. She flopped off-balance, hands flailed across the dented hood, grabbing for a hold. Uncertain whether she could slap or scratch a reverend, she twisted toward the front bumper.

Preacher clamped a liver-spotted hand across her mouth. Fumbling, he ripped her dress buttons, grabbed her tits, and yanked her skirt up, wadding it around her waist. He fumbled a moment with his pants, then snatched her head back by her hair, and bent her across the ancient front wheel well. Too flaccid from drink and unable to push into her, he slammed her to her knees and shoved her face into his crotch. He ground across her mouth, holding her head tight.

She struggled to stand, pushed against him as she felt his member swell and heard him panting. He flopped her onto her belly and fell onto generous buttocks, knocking her breathless. Moaning, he spent himself onto her bare bottom, then shoved her away, pulled his pants up, and staggered back, pointing at her.

"You a handmaiden. Remember that. A hand-maiden."

Opening the dust-covered cab, he sprawled face down onto a tattered seat, ragged snores rising immediately. Mosquitoes settled on his face and arms.

Lisa slid down the wheel well and knelt next to the truck, sobbing. She stared ruefully at the prone figure, legs dangling out the door.

"Mama, Mama, why do you shove men on me? Especially this preacher. This ain't Christian guidance." Snot and tears streamed down her face. Heartsick and frightened, she stood, wadded ripped panties into a tight ball, stuffed them in her pocket, and straightened her dress. The bodice was ripped and two buttons were missing.

Not the first time someone assumed that it was OK to mistreat me because I'm fat. Not the first time Mama promised me away and pushed me toward some man. Not the first time for that. First time for a preacher man.

Crying, she stumbled through the camp-ground to the river's edge, waded into a gentle eddy and plopped down. Breathing in deep heaves, she sat for a time with her face in her hands.

Gathering herself, she sloshed cold liquid on her butt, inner thighs, and hair-covered mound. She sucked in a deep breath and ducked under the current.

If only I could stay cradled here forever.

She felt weightless. Her hair floated in a graceful pirouette. Her ears rang and throat tightened. She felt the heavy thump of her heart. No sense saying anything to anyone about this little set-to. She knew Preacher was an itinerant man that came for river baptisms and revival camp meetings. He offered the tiny community salvation and a break in their monotonous hardscrabble lives. Folks simply overlooked his shortcomings. Besides, her mother pushed her into the man's clutches, using her, once again, for some hidden purpose.

Unable to hold her breath longer, she sat up and gasped, humid air filled her straining lungs. Resting her elbows on her knees, she coughed in deep spasms.

Startled, an owl lifted off a dead limb and glided silently into the dark. Night creatures rustled in the weeds. The river whispered south. She sat a long time listening to the life around her.

Her breathing steadied. The violent pumping of her heart slowed.

Next day, Preacher never even glanced at Lisa Dell. He knelt on the embankment bent over, praying real hard. He looked less like a preacher than a black crane feeding on some frog hidden in the cattails. Finally, he rose, arms uplifted, and eyed the knot of believers.

Hot as it was, Lisa shivered. Up the bank, families and community members croaked through "Take Me to the Water" slightly off key.

"You people, brothers and sisters in the Lord, come on down to the river with me." Preacher's nostrils flared as he spoke, making his hooked nose appear capable of sniffing out sinful thoughts. His eyes lent him the look of an angel-possessed avenger wielding a flaming sword against evil in men's souls. A thin aura of tarnished glory settled across his bony shoulders. The reek of liquor lingered about him.

"Sing again, fellow Christians. Lift up your voices and tell these folks they will be saved." He gestured toward the group of converts.

The gathering broke into "We Shall Gather at the River," their voices earnestly grabbing at a rough harmony, struggling with just the right key.

"Ain't you been baptized before?" Lisa Dell whispered to a wrinkled, sun-darkened spinster standing next to her.

"Girl, I like for Preacher to put me in the river ever time he comes through. Only time I gets any attention."

"Attention?" She thought a minute. "Don't matter that you done been washed? Ain't this for God?"

"No, girl. I ain't doing it for Him. I do it for me. Preacher never seems to mind neither. He jes' likes to baptize folks. 'Specially womenfolk." She spat a stream of tobacco juice onto the sand and carefully wiped her mouth. "Seem like Jesus takes us all any way we come, any time."

A sandy-haired boy nearby snickered. "Know what? If I 'as big as you I'd be real worried. Preacher cain't duck no cow."

Angry at the boy's mean-spirited taunt, her mother's desperation, and the conniving self-gratification of the preacher, Lisa Dell spun around.

"For someone about to be baptized, saved from sin and full of heavenly love, you saying some dirt-mean things," she hissed. "In fact, that's ugly talk from Satan hisself."

"Ain't neither, 'cause it's true. You ought to be scared about getting dropped and drowning." The boy snorted.

"Preacher too skinny to be holding you up. He humped you pretty good other night though. I know 'cause I watched."

"You egg sucking white trash. You don't know nuthin. I ain't standing near you and your evil, spiteful tongue."

"You one needs to worry. Heck, Preacher know you don't believe. He heard talk about you."

"He might a' heard. But he told me I'm saved and can serve as a handmaiden like Hagar. My mama prayed with Preacher. He told me I needed to give myself to him 'cause he's Jesus Christ's messenger on earth."

The boy hooted. "That's another way of saying he can poke you for free. You sin when you lay with a man not your husband. Jes' 'cause he's a preacher don't make no difference."

Tears welled up in Lisa's eyes. She elbowed him aside and stomped defiantly to the end of the line. Sniffing, she gathered her white dress around her generous bosom. A sodden breeze wafted across her face.

Preacher stood a moment on the bank intoning. He prayed. He began another sermon.

"You are buried in water with Christ and your sins washed away, white as garments you wear. You will emerge clean and filled with light." His voice rose.

"I hold the key to your everlasting life here in my hands, in this river. Lord said that unless man is born of water and the Spirit, he cannot enter the Kingdom of God. He that believes is saved."

He took off his black frock coat, waded waist deep into the swamp-fed river and waved people forward. Several deacons inched into the water and stood knee deep, helping lead supplicants toward a wider channel.

Preacher smiled, grasped each petitioner, drew them close and placed a hand-held cloth over their faces, pressing each beneath tea-colored water.

"In the name of the Father, Son and Holy Ghost, I baptize you. Your sins are washed away. Walk in life renewed."

Lisa Dell hung back. She fidgeted, thinking.

If mother told me to lay with Preacher, and Preacher said I would serve as a handmaiden, was it really a sin of fornication? If he forced himself on me, what was that? My sin or his? What about honoring my mother and doing what she told me? How much can a river wash away?

Doubts fluttered through her mind. No sense turning back now. She'd spent days and nights here with these people, working and singing and caring for their children. Preacher had forced himself on her and that felt bad wrong. No matter. Still, baptizing always transformed a riotous revival week into a final sweet day of forgiveness and renewal.

Last in line, she stepped forward and waded out. For his part, Parson licked his lips at the sight of her full body moving through the warm river.

In one motion, he clamped a claw-like hand around her wrist, pulled her to his side, and rubbed his leg across her privates. He placed his free hand over her face and submersed her.

Water rushed over her body, causing her to gasp. Had it not been for the cloth, she would've fallen into a coughing fit.

"In the name of the Father, Son and the Holy Ghost, I baptize you. You are a daughter of God, carry the word with you."

He lifted her up. His hand slid off her face,

down her neck, and slyly pinched her breasts. Again, he placed the cloth on her face and pushed her beneath the water.

"Put your trust in God. You are washed free of sin," he said loudly to the knot of believers. "Life starts new for you."

Lifting her up for a second time, he smiled and whispered in her ear. "You a handmaiden of God with a rich body. Share it."

Unnerved by his whispers, his callous feeling of her body, and her own conflicted, blasphemous thoughts, she struggled against his groping. Gasping, she misstepped, floundered in bottom mud, and fell backward. Her ritual dress billowed out and swamped them both.

Preacher grabbed at her. Struggling, the two sank into deeper water. A great whirlpool swirled about their bodies and gathered up past and future wickedness in one fluid motion.

Sputtering, they clawed to the surface, only to gag and drag each other down thrashing. Silt rose in dark clouds and obscured their struggles.

The gaggle along the bank stood transfixed and aghast. Finally, a deacon and several community members waded out. One grabbed at

Lisa Dell's flailing arms, intent on pulling her to firm footing. Another snatched at her sack dress, tried to wrap his hand in the hem, and haul her up the bank. Instead, everyone sank in a morass of snorts.

Another fella splashed in and tossed a rope to the struggling group. One man grabbed the hemp lifeline, and then another latched on, and, finally, Lisa Dell caught ahold.

Hauled to firm footing, she coughed violently, rotund body heaving, wet hair plastered her face and channeled rivulets into her eyes. Bent over, hands on her knees, she fought to catch her breath. Her breasts hung loose in magnificent pendulums. The cotton dress precisely outlined her full body. Confused and ashamed, she stumbled toward people on the bank as the deacons turned to help Preacher.

A thin farmer stepped forward, glared through bushy eyebrows, and pointed a grime-caked finger at her.

"Girl, you laid with Preacher and the river rejected you. That's God's way of punishing your sin. Jezebel. Harlot. Whore."

Murmurs and whispers ghosted about. Some folks nodded agreement, others stepped back and shook their heads.

"Preacher's a man of God and you tempted him. You are damned."

"That ain't for you to say. Jesus Christ forgave the harlot, forgave Mary Magdalene. He be the one going to judge," intoned a withered crone.

"It weren't like that," Lisa Dell said. "Preacher told me I'm like a handmaiden. My mama pushed me forward same as Sarah did Hagar."

"God judges. Leave that girl be," said a young mother, toddler balanced on her hip. "That preacher man is lustful." Red faced, she turned and scurried away. Several other women nodded agreement.

Lisa stared at the knot of people then turned and watched parson, frantic and alone, as he surfaced slightly downstream. Catching a dead tree limb, he pulled himself toward the main trunk.

Buttons gone, his shirt hung open exposing a fish-belly white chest. His suspenders, ripped off thin shoulders by the current, hung askew about his hips. He struggled, hand-by-hand, up the fallen tree until he could crawl up the bank.

Obligingly, the river washed away the smell of whiskey. A taint of sin lingered.

Lisa plopped down on coarse sand, trembling.

Children stood with mouths open and gawked. A baby cried. Some folks turned away, grim faced, and whispered. Others, like moths drawn to a flame, edged closer. Finally, a knobby hand patted her head, wrapped a thin towel around her shoulders, and pulled her to standing.

"Girl, you need to go on now. No sense worrying over what cain't be undone. Lord works in strange ways. Trust Him. You done been washed in the water."

During the night, Preacher left out for his next calling. Mama went with him. A neighbor woman said she heard Mama say as a respectable white woman, she promised she'd help him gather new converts. Lisa thought that would be mostly young females. Her mama never even said good-bye.

Alone and on her own for the first time, Lisa Dell felt a lightness of being. Pure and simple, she thought, this baptism was a sign, an omen, a turning point. Washed clean in the water, she felt a new beginning take root.

Without a backward glance, she started off down the dusty road.

The Day the Snake Got Killed

~~~~~~

The tiny green body writhed, exposing a pale white-yellow belly. Twisting over and over, dark eyes unblinking, it flashed a forked tongue and thrashed, helpless. The three children gawked.

Elvoy, oldest at age fifteen, had located the snake under umbrella-shaped squash leaves, snapped it out by its tail, whacked it with a stick, and flung the small form toward Billman.

The child let loose with a single high screech, whirled around, stumped his toe on a stob, and sprawled face down. Still screaming, he scrambled out of the garden on all fours. At the edge of the yard, he realized the snake had landed among green beans. Standing up, he snuffed, rubbed his skint knee, and attempted to recover his seven-year-old male dignity.

Dissolving in guffaws, Elvoy bent over and clutched his stomach. A slender, bony fellow, he sprang from a clan of white trash who survived near a palmetto hammock. His people hunted and trapped without regard to any law. They caught live rattlers and gators and sold them to gas stations and tourist courts as roadside attractions. Travelers on their way to Miami or Fort Lauderdale liked to stop, lean over snake pits or crocodile ponds, and throw empty Coke bottles, rocks, and other debris at the hapless reptiles in an attempt to incite some action.

"Chop his head off! Use this here grubber." Elvoy taunted both younger children. He grabbed a hoe propped on the fence and shoved it on Sissy. "Do it. Chop his head off! It ain't nuthin' but a snake."

"It's harmless." Sissy shook her head and backed away.

"No, it ain't. Make you sicker than a dog if it bites."

They watched the garden snake struggle. Billman, on the edge of the drama, wiped his nose and inched back cautious-like toward them.

"Do it. Do like I tell you." Elvoy's eyes narrowed. He sneered at Sissy. "You chicken. You yellow pussy chicken."

"No. I'm not going to. You're chicken. Besides, it's harmless," she said.

The tall boy pushed Sissy sideways. She stumbled, fell and scraped her hands in coarse sand. She glared at the dirty, overalls-clad figure standing over her.

He stared down and thumped a stick in his callused palm. She wiped her nose, scrambled up, grabbed the hoe, and shoved it back at him.

"Do it your own self."

"You do it." He stood splay-legged before her. "I double dog dare you to do it Miss-teacher's-pet too-goody-pants," he snarled, stained teeth practically snapping. "Do it or I'm gonna whack ya 'side yer head." He stepped toward her, stick raised.

Sunlight caught the arc of the hoe as Sissy slashed downward, chopping a small head away from its writhing green body. She stared and stood watching its final death twitches.

"Sissy! Child! What are you doing?"

Grandma's voice cut through humid air as clean as the blade had sliced off the snake's head. Screen slapped against the back door frame as the rotund woman stomped down creaking porch steps and marched across a hard-pack yard toward the garden. Billman began screaming again. Knuckles white, Sissy clutched the hoe and stood wide eyed.

"He said he'd hit me if I didn't kill it. He shoved me down. Besides it was dying anyway."

Grandma glowered. She wiped her hands on her apron, firmly took the hoe from Sissy and eye-balled the older boy.

"Elvoy, you got no upbringing, living among all those bloody relations of yours, but that's no excuse. I knew your mama before she got lost with that trash, and she was a good woman. I know she taught you better. At least she tried to. For her sake, I'll not do anything further." She pointed her gnarled finger at the skinny boy, her voice hard.

"I'll let it go just this once. But, don't you ever come here again. You take your meanness and git."

"It was a snake. A slimy snake. Yer jes' trying to put ever-thang on me. She one done kilt it." The boy backed up and started edging out of the yard. "Bible says snake tempted Adam in Garden of

Eden. Snakes and women. They evil." He wheeled, sprinted through palmetto scrub, and disappeared.

Hands on her hips, the woman turned toward the girl and crying boy. A sodden breeze blew across the three figures. In the distance, a black crow cawed and bobbed up and down on a fence post.

"Billman, you hush your howling. Sissy, pick up this little thing. Go bury it. Put him at the end of the tomato row." She gestured toward the garden. "You've killed my emerald prince whose only crime was being a snake. At least he can rest in the garden where he lived."

"I'm sorry. I'm sorry. I didn't really mean to hurt it." Sissy started crying. Billman, seeing her tears, wound up again and squalled.

"And how do you propose to not hurt something when you're chopping at it with a hoe? A life is a precious thing and should not be taken just because you have the power. Why this little thing ate crickets and grasshoppers for me. Go on now and bury him."

They stared down at the still body. Sissy rubbed her hands on her shorts and looked up at her grandmother.

"I'm sorry. I'm sorry. I didn't mean to hurt your snake."

"Y'all hurry now. Do like I tell you. Then come in the house. I need help taking food to Alberta."

Sighing, the woman turned away. Her huge bosom heaved. Pulling a handkerchief out of her bra, she dabbed sweat from her upper lip, and strode up wooden steps, shaking her head. Grey wisps of hair floated free about her wrinkled face. Opening the screen door, she disappeared into the kitchen.

Grandma pulled a cured ham, crowned by brown sugar glaze and pineapple rings, out of the oven. Carefully, she placed it on a crockery platter and covered it with tin foil. Dark smoke-spice scents wafted through the kitchen.

"Girl, you put those sweet potatoes and beans in some bowls while I make up a batch of biscuits. Get that cardboard box off the back porch and start packing this food up for Alberta."

"Why do you do this? Don't she cook?"

"It's Lord's Acre Day at church. In case you forgot, that's a sharing time. Besides, you know she needs help feeding those children. Without her husband, she can barely make ends meet. Especially since old man Hendrick threw them out of the sharecropper cabin."

"But they live way down in the quarters. 'Sides, she just sits there, staring and rocking."

"I know. Quit chattering and get busy. Be sure you put in that jug of sweet tea and those deviled eggs."

Rows of shotgun cabins lined a pot-holed dirt road, muddy in wet weather and dust shrouded in dry. Sissy bounced along in the blue Ford with Grandma, staring out a half-opened window. The old woman wrestled the grumbling car down a rut-scarred street. Grooves wrenched the sedan from one side to another.

Dark children stopped playing and watched its jerking progress. Knotty old men lounged near shanty beer joints or sat sullenly on wooden stoops and whittled. Withered crones silently propped against a clapboard wall or stepped from some yawning doorway into glaring afternoon sun. Young men and nubile women challenged the small troop's progress with sassy laughter and bold, swaying hips as they moved between dogtrot shacks or crossed the sand track.

Dust roiled up as Grandma stopped before a dilapidated, rusted tin-roof shack. She set the hand brake, slung the car door open, and stepped smartly toward the trunk.

"Girl, come help me tote this stuff in. Mind your manners."

"Yes'm."

Sissy opened her door and shyly stepped out into powder-fine red dust. A gaggle of children collected at the edge of the porch. Wide eyes staring out of dark faces, they watched.

Grandma lifted a box of food and started toward the house.

"You bring that tea." She nodded at the trunk and turned, gesturing with her head for Sissy to follow. She stopped beside the steps and carefully placed the food box on the stoop.

"Here's dinner for you and the family. I hope you like butter beans and ham."

"We shore do, Miz Mildred. We 'preciate y'alls thinking of us." The black woman's voice carried a flat note of polite deference.

"My sister done give up since her man gone. Don't seem right. Him going off with the Army to fight that there war in Italy. It were on some river.

The Arnie or sumthin like that there. Then he come home and them swamp trash lynched him." Blame curdled beneath her words.

"Too uppity in his uniform they said."

"I know. I know." The large woman stood a moment looking at the hardscrabble shacks and the black faces that carefully reflected nothing.

"I'm sorry for your loss. Seems like there's too much meanness in the world. Too much for women-folk to clean up and hold straight."

"Yes, ma'am. We grateful *you* got a conscience. Lord's Acre Day and y'all comed over. Seems like you feels better and us eats good. At least today."

The black woman nodded at the white one. For a brief moment, their eyes met, acknowledged shared grief, saying everything, saying nothing, and then slid apart.

The self-imposed errand completed, Grandma wrestled her car around, grinding gears and stalling out as ruts grabbed the tires. Finally, she got headed back home across the railroad tracks. Dust ropes marked their progress toward town.

"Grandma, that woman says same thing every time we come. Why does she do that?"

"Miss Mattie to you. She's Alberta's sister and I'll

have you speak to them and about them with respect."

"Yes'm. But why does she always say the same thing?"

"Because it's important." She paused. "Because it still hurts and she wants to remind us."

"We didn't do it though."

"Our kind did. White folks. Trash with meanness in their souls."

"Like Elvoy? And that snake?"

"Sort of."

By the time Grandma got home, evening shadows crept along the kitchen floor. A single, bare bulb hung over the sink by an electric umbilical cord. She clicked the light on and began supper. Mixing fresh cornbread, she slipped it in the oven, washed and cleaned turnips and greens, and threw them in a pot with ham scraps.

"Grandma! Billman and me found you another snake. It's in the corncrib." A slamming door punctuated Sissy's announcement.

"It's got all colors on it. It's real pretty. What kind do you think it is?"

"I don't know. Let's go look." The older woman dried her hands and followed Sissy.

Billman stood holding a weathered plank door

open, dancing from one foot to another. Several speckled hens scratched around the stacked rock footing, clucking as they looked for loose grain. Light filtered through cracks between crib boards.

A small red, black and yellow banded snake lay coiled atop a corn pile. Tongue flicking in and out, it paused a moment, then slid through brown husks, glided around a cast iron sheller, and disappeared. Dust motes danced in a shaft of late afternoon sun.

"Why it looks like a rat snake," Grandma said. "They have similar coloring to a coral snake but are harmless. Unless you're a rat. Then you might get swallowed."

"That's right! I remember now," said Sissy. "Teacher told us 'red and yellow, kill a fellow; red and black, friend of Jack.'"

"Teacher told me rat snakes are better than cats about catching mice," Billman shyly offered.

"Don't you ever tell nobody about this here snake. It's Grandma's new snake," Sissy said. "We'll keep it for her. You hear?" She stared hard at her brother before turning back toward the plump form.

"Does this make up for killing the green one?" Sissy's voice caught and her bottom lip trembled.

The boy cut eyes up at his grandma and stood as close as possible.

Sighing, she put a hand on Sissy's head and gently stroked it.

"No. No, it does not. You can't undo what's been done. Remember that. You can only keep going and do better next time. For right now, let's go in and finish supper."

The children jumped out of the corn crib, closed its door, and slipped the wooden latch into place. The kitchen light threw a soft yellow glow across the porch.

The Cane Grinding

∿∿∿∿∿∿∿∿∿∿∿∿∿∿∿∿∿∿∿∿∿∿∿∿∿∿∿∿∿∿∿∿∿∿

Late Saturday afternoon, Sarah watched as Mama, Pap and Martha Ann with Baby Blue piled into the decrepit Ford pickup. They rattled off down the road in a rooster tail of dust toward old man Chesterfield's cane sugar mill.

Mama's instructions rang in her ears: finish the ironing, do the milking, gather eggs, and then walk on down to the neighboring farm.

Deliberately, Sarah lingered over the ironing board humming to herself, dawdled around gathering eggs, and strolled down to fetch Belle from the pasture for evening milking. Milk sloshed out as Sarah carried the pail to the house, stopping on the way to pour some into a shallow pan for the barn cats. They ringed about, a pinwheel of stripes and colors, jostling against each other.

Chores finished, Sarah washed her face, pulled on a clean shirt, and glanced in the mirror. A narrow face and dark brown eyes stared back. Although Mama called the freckles splattered across her nose good luck pennies, she knew they were simply brown spots. But truth be told, she realized she was fence post plain and that most folks simply looked around her, never *seeing* her.

As day reluctantly loosened its grip and night encroached, Sarah dared not piddle around any longer. Ambling down the dirt track, she scuffed her feet through warm, coarse sand. Fireflies sparkled in purple dusk beneath moss shawls of live oaks. Birds twittered and squabbled, settling for the night. An insect chorus rose and throbbed to a deafening hosanna.

Sarah loved syrup making since it was one of the few non-church social gatherings in her rural community. She played king-of-the-hill with other youngsters on the cane pummy pile, running, jumping, and shoving with abandon. But, since getting her period, Mama forbade any more tumbling around, especially with boys. Now, she hung around women with their homespun, earthy wisdom and, occasionally, around men talking tobacco and hog prices.

At fourteen, she had a stick figure, flat chest, chewed-off fingernails, and limp stringy hair, not much to attract the fellers, even married ones that hankered to run their hands over someone besides their own wife. At school, she felt different from other girls as they whispered and giggled about their kissing and groping adventures.

Despite feeling alone and different, school was nonetheless her refuge. Her teacher, Miss Rebecca, bragged on Sarah's reading and spelling, book reports, and even math. Miss Rebecca encouraged her to work hard in school, go on to state college and make something of herself. Never quite sure exactly what that meant, Sarah relished the attention.

By the time she stepped into the weak light surrounding the syrup mill yard, night had tossed a soft cloak over the gathering. The cooking shed, with its stout oak posts and tin roof, stood open to the air. A great cast iron kettle sat on a brick throne. Cane juice bubbled, simmered, and changed from a watery greenish hue to a thick sable brown. Old man Chesterfield and his field hand Moses stirred and tended the fire, keeping it hot enough to cook juice down but not so hot as to scorch.

Nancy Hartney

Women, talking in slow, easy voices, sat scattered under the shed.

No sooner had she propped herself against a post, than Martha Ann spotted her.

"Come on over and take this here baby." Her voice had a sharp edge. "I don't know what took you so long to walk down here."

Her sister had chestnut hair and two melon-round breasts, her greatest assets. She was eight years older than Sarah, just enough to give her more than big sister rank.

Sarah didn't mind the baby, but she resented her sister's demands. She felt used.

"You're Blue's mama. You do it."

"Do what I say. You ain't so big that I cain't smack you." Sighing, Sarah shuffled over and took the baby.

"Martha Ann, he's wet. Why you give him to me nasty?"

"It don't seem to bother him none. Just stop whining and hold him awhile. I been stuck with him this entire afternoon."

"Well, he's yours. You supposed to take care of him."

"All you gonna do is sit. Besides, sister dearie,

you his aunt." Martha Ann stood, hands on her hips and stuck her breasts out. "You mind being so *kind* as to help me a little? I got to go over yonder to see Jackson."

"Jackson? What about Zack Winston Morris? Ain't he Baby Blue's daddy? You done spoke for. At least that's what you *said*."

"Well, he's off working sawmills over to Arkansas. Soon's he gets money, he be back." She cut her eyes around at the lanky fellow unhitching the mill mule.

"Jackson's his best friend so he'll keep an eye on me. And, baby. Helping us all he can. Leastwise, I think that's what Zack wants him to do."

Sarah glared at her sister. No sense talking to her when her hussy side set eyes on a man or wanted to shove work off on someone. Resentful, she held the baby and watched as Martha Ann, hips swaying, minced off.

Snatches of talk drifted toward Sarah as she watched her sister sidle up to the old mule, hook her fingers in the harness, and smile coyly across at the man.

"Y'all need help, Jackson?"

"Sure thing, Martha Ann." He grinned. "I'm

takin' this here molly down to feed her."

Sarah watched. Jackson unhitched the stoic mule from the sweep arm and led her toward a dilapidated outbuilding. Martha Ann rubbed against him as they ambled toward the barn door.

Once again, Sarah felt used and ignored. She stood a long minute, then whirled and marched into the cooking lean-to and gossipy snatches of talk humming among the women.

After a bit, tired of Blue and curious about Martha Ann, she stood up and stepped toward her mother.

"Mama, will you hold this baby? My arms got tired, and I need to let my water go. Besides, he's gone to sleep."

"Did you change him?" Her mother frowned.

"Yes ma'am, I did." Sarah felt a pang of guilt. Mama looked worn down. After all, she had raised three boys, two girls, lost two other infants, and worked a dirt farm sunrise to sunset for forty years. She had no hankering to take on a grand-baby. Especially from an unmarried daughter not inclined to work.

"Bring that Blue to me. I'll holt him a spell." An old crone cackled from the corner, took one last dip of snuff, settled into a cane-bottom chair, and held out her stringy arms. "You young heifers got no more notion 'bout caring for a little one than a cat does." She rocked gently, pausing occasionally to spit a viscous stream into dust powder surrounding the shed.

Freed of the baby, Sarah strode to the dry lot where the mule stood quietly chewing hay. She slipped under the board fence, found a spot, squatted and peed. Finished, she pulled her panties up.

Curiosity took over, so she stooped down and peeked through a crack in the plank barn. A milk cow, standing near a hay mound, chewed her cud. Chickens, gone to roost on barn rafters, fussed and bickered softly. Shadows sprawled across a dirt floor.

Low grunts drew her attention. There, in the last stall, she vaguely made out Jackson standing against Martha Ann. He pawed at her clothes. She giggled, moved her hips against his crotch, kissed him, and rubbed her hands through his hair.

Jackson unbuckled his pants, reared back, lifted Martha Ann and braced her against the barn wall. She moaned, clamped her legs around his waist, and hiked her skirt up. With all the grinding and banging, Jackson's loose pants slipped down around his ankles.

Fascinated, Sarah watched the two figures grunt against each other. Prickly shivers ran up her arms and across her scalp. So this was what those older girls in the school yard snickered about. Looked like a cross between messy groping and pit-of–your-stomach goose bumps thrilling. Still in all, she knew bragging rights got attached to it.

Pondering hard, Sarah walked back toward the hum of voices and syrup-house light. As she neared the cane pile, a teasing voice floated toward her.

"You ain't no looker, is you?"

She stopped, squinted her eyes against the light, and peered into the dark. A figure stood at the edge of the pummy pile.

"You not much your own self, Jim Guy Hermann," she retorted.

"Girl, you don't need worry about my looks. There's plenty gals around after me."

"No they ain't." Sarah smirked. "Besides, I know Saturday afternoons your pa and y'all boys get drunk on 'shine from Tindal's. You end up on your butt nowheres near a girl. Besides, you wouldn't know what to do if one jumped right on you."

"Hush your mouth. At least I don't have no hussy cow for a sister."

"Take that back you sorry egg sucker." Defiant, Sarah strode up to him and thrust her face forward. "What do you know about anything anyway? You nothing but an ignorant peckerwood."

"You nuthin' but a teacher's pet. A suck-up." His hands shot toward her, shoving her backward. She stumbled awkwardly, struggled to keep her balance, slipped on the crushed cane stalks, and fell hard on her bottom. He pounced on top, pinned her arms with his knees and laughed. She bucked and struggled against his awkward groping and sloppy efforts at kissing.

They scuffed about, kicking and tussling, until their clothes got tangled into wads between them.

Jim Guy, fighting overalls, zippers, and buttons, gave up. Inexperienced, sweating, and out of breath, he sprawled beside her.

"Not much to look at, but for a girl you sure enough strong."

She stared at him. Girls at school talked about him like he was some kinda prize. He did have coal-dark hair and water-blue eyes. But his crooked teeth and bad breath made her gag. Besides, he wore greasy overalls and had cob-rough hands. Worse yet, she knew the Hermann family lived on top of each other in a dogtrot house deep in the palmetto scrub, adding to their litter with a new baby every year. Hermann men, known to prefer fishing and hunting, obligingly left any work to their women. Not something she wanted.

She stared at him. Emboldened, Jim Guy sat up and kissed her smack on the mouth. A clumsy, slug-tongue-down-her-throat kiss.

Glaring, Sarah pushed him away and rolled to standing. Disgusted, she wiped her hand across her mouth.

She'd been kissed. Her *first* kiss. Damn. No goose bumps. Turned out to be slobber and spit. Sarah spun around and stalked off toward the cook shed. Blushing, she sat in shadows next to old granny.

"Girl, you better come back up here. I seen that boy grab you and y'all roll around on them stalks." The old woman smiled knowingly.

"Best be sure you keep your panties on and your legs crossed. No sense inviting misery into your life with stuff a man brings."

Sarah stared at granny's browned face, spider-webbed from years in the sun. The crone nodded and patted her arm with gnarled, deformed fingers.

"You take on a man and next thing you know, you done birthed a baby. Don't mean nothing 'cause you still got to go in them tobacco fields. Get done there, you got to finish up yard chores and feed him and raise that baby." The crone continued to rock and hold the sleeping child.

"Now you might think that sister of yours is real pretty. That ain't gonna last. Between hoeing cotton, pulling tobacco, slopping hogs and having a baby ever' year, she'll wash right out." Granny shifted and continued rocking. "Womenfolks usually gets short end of the stick."

Her mouth agape, Sarah nodded. "They not all like that, are they? Can't women do something else?"

"What do you think? What do you want?"

"Well, my school teacher, Miss Rebecca? She's from St. Louis and she told me to go to state college. Said I could get off the farm. See some sights."

"Maybe best listen to that teacher." The old

woman put a pinch of snuff in her bottom lip. "Come to think of it, I hear tell Doc's nurse gonna move to a hospital in Mobile come February. Got a fancy job there. Follow her example."

"Mobile, Alabama." Sarah tasted excitement as she rolled the words around on her tongue. "That's a big city with lights and cars and all kinds of stores." Eagerness crept into her voice. "You know that lady at the bank? She's taking mail order schooling. She tells me and Mama about it when we go in on Saturdays. She says she plans on being an accountant. Maybe I could do that."

Angry sounds shattered Sarah's thoughts. Talk among women at the cook shed stopped. The knot of men standing in the firelight grew quiet. All heads turned, listening to jagged-sharp voices spilling out of the barn.

"Damn sumbitch. Get the hell away from her."

Zack Winston Morris, finally come home to see Martha Ann and his son Blue, stood at the entrance to the barn, legs splayed apart, and fists clenched.

"You damn cow. I work my butt off at them saw camps and get home to find you humping my best friend."

Zack spun away from Martha Ann, stepped forward, and swung his fist full into Jackson's face. Blood sprayed across both boys.

"Damn it all. You done gone and busted my nose," Jackson howled. "How come you do that?"

"Well, what the hell I supposed to do? I come home and find you with my wife." Zack worked himself up into a slobbering fit.

Jackson, dripping blood, mumbled through his hand. "She ain't your wife. Y'all never stood up with no preacher. Y'all ain't churched. Till you do, that baby don't mean she yer wife." He wiped red mucus off on his pants. "Sides, I was jes' helping her."

"She don't need no help."

Martha Ann, struggling into her clothes, hollered while the fellers stiff-legged around like banty roosters.

With a crowd arriving, both men flailed away at each other for the sake of appearances. Two black eyes, a broken tooth, and a busted lip later, they lay exhausted on the ground, blood splattered and grunting at each other.

"Gawd damn you, Zack. You ought to tolt us you coming home."

"That gonna keep you from jumping my woman?"

"I told you, I wuz trying to keep her content till you could get back. I know she's yours and I ain't trying to get between y'all."

"Hell you say. You poking her not gettin' between us?"

"I never meant it to. Honest to gawd, ain't meant it to." He rolled to standing and offered a hand down to Zack.

"She kept making eyes at me and then come down here in the barn rubbing all over me. I didn't tell her to come. I swear." Jackson appeared contrite.

"You lying stump-jumper." Martha Ann's voice oozed anger. "You the one that kept whispering and trying to feel my tits ever since Zack done left."

Martha Ann glared at Jackson, strode up, and cracked him across his face. Her perfect hand print glowed ugly on his cheek.

She spun around on Zack. "You never even asked me about going to no preacher. Minute you find out I'm gonna have a baby, you zipped up your britches and took off. You worthless piece of redneck trash." She reared back and laid a stinging wallop on him.

Several of the women gasped, and then nodded, remembering the times they were discounted and betrayed by others. Some of the men hollered out loud, gleeful at any possibility of a three-way fight.

Martha Ann turned toward the crowd, hands on her hips, and poked her great bosom out defiantly. Wisps of hay clung in her hair.

"What y'all gawking at? This none of y'alls business."

The two fellers glanced at each other, surprised. They shuffled about, ducked their heads, and rubbed the sting out of Martha's slap.

"Gawd, Zack. You and me know'd each other before she even come around. We huntin' partners. Drinkin' buddies. Come on. This is nothing. Let's go by Tindal's place, see we find some white dog. Forget this thing. She ain't worth it. No woman is."

Zack looked from Martha Ann to Jackson and back. He shrugged, stooped, picked up his hat and slouched up the hill away from the crowd. Jackson licked his lip, adjusted his britches, and trailed behind his friend.

Shaking their heads, women ambled back to

the bubbling syrup with memories of lost beauty and misspent loving twisting through their thoughts. Men stood awhile scratching, spitting, chuckling, and telling tales of their own misdeeds and male adventures.

Sarah gawked in disbelief at the two fellers' disappearing backs. She glanced over at Blue gurgling happily, blissfully unaware of any fracas.

Turning around, she spotted Jim Guy sidling up to Jackson and Zack, making like he was invited to go along.

Martha Ann finished adjusting her blouse, marched toward the crone, and all but snatched the baby. Stomping up to the truck, she climbed in and slammed the door. And there she sat, as far away from wagging tongues and smirks as she could manage.

Close on after midnight, cane juice had simmered down into a consistency for dripping and bottling. The kettle fire died to a smoldering ash heap and a dark-sweet odor lingered heavy under the rafters.

The granny appeared content to rock and dip her snuff. Sarah, twisting a wisp of hair around her finger, sat next to her, and glanced sideways at the old woman.

"You reckon you got to have a man to get on? You reckon I can live some place other than the farm? Like Atlanta? Or Birmingham? Be on my own? Least ways for a little while? I'd like to *see* a big city."

"Girl, I don't know. Seems to me folks get anxious and takes whatever they see. Vinegar gets to running in them and they don't look much past what they can grab right here and now. They settle for less. Pretty soon hopes dry up like morning dew and they don't even *remember* dreams. They gets too dragged out. You got to hold on to yourself and not lose them ideas."

"Sarah, you come on now," Mama hollered. "We might as well go on to the house. Most folks already left on out. 'Sides, Chesterfield and Moses can finish off last of the syrup."

They walked toward their rusty truck. Martha Ann still sat in the cab fuming, her lips pressed into a thin bitter line. Baby Blue, sound asleep, never stirred when Mama and Pap climbed in.

Off in the distance, a barn owl hooted. A pearl moon threw shadows across the road. Pines swayed in a night breeze, whispering secrets hidden in human hearts. A hint of autumn floated gentle on the air.

After several cranks the ancient truck rattled to life. With grown-ups in front, Sarah climbed in back and hunched down against the cab.

The Fig Trees

~~~~~~

Mama's honey-slow voice floated from the kitchen accompanied by a tinkle of spoons and aroma of perked coffee.

"Child, stop your piddling around and hurry. The bus'll be here soon."

"I know Mama. I'm hurrying."

Lee rolled out of her sagging bed, nightgown wadded around her stick figure. She yawned, stretched, and shuffled barefooted across the cool pine floors to the closet-sized bathroom.

She splashed water on her face, combed the sleep-tangles out of her hair, and padded back to the bedroom. Wiggling into a homemade dress, she pulled on bobby socks, and slipped into brown saddle oxfords. She stared in the mirror. Stringy dishwater colored hair. Fingernails chewed to the quick. Plain as an old corn cob. Never mind she thought. School's starting and summer tobacco season finished.

She plopped down at the kitchen table, grabbed an oven-warm buttermilk biscuit and smeared on fig preserves.

Mama bustled between the gas stove and a sink of soapy water. Drying her hands on a flour-sack apron, she leaned out the back door, and looked down the dirt road.

"I see it coming. It's already at the Watson's farm. You'll have to run."

"Yes, Mama." Lee scrambled up from the table and grabbed her notebook and pencils.

"Don't forget, ride home with Grace Harris after school. She's coming to pick figs."

"You already told me that. I'll remember." The screen door slapped closed as Lee sprinted out.

The yellow bus rocked to a stop in a dust maelstrom. She clambered aboard and the old vehicle lurched forward, grumbling on toward the county school.

Gangly and shy, Lee sat in the back alone. She thought about her new teacher and classes. Parched farms slid past the rattling bus windows.

Cold in winter and hot as summer came on, the leaky cinder block building stood near the railroad tracks across the county road. Every few years, the board saw fit to have the peeling concrete repainted white, the roof patched, and the gym floor varnished because the boys' basketball team was the pride of the county. Still, an aura of faded hope echoed in the structure's stark corridors.

The bus ground to a stop and disgorged a chattering, flowing crush of students as the opening bell clanged.

Lee hated the jostling for homeroom seats. Every year, school unrolled the same. Rowdy athletes grabbed the back places, prissy town girls strategically positioned themselves between teacher and the basketball players, while nondescript farm kids took the middle section.

A front row desk near the windows stood empty. Again. She settled into the wobbly seat. A chameleon girl, she blended into any setting and most groups by default. Even when there, no one noticed.

Lee loved the rhythm of classes, her haven away from the hardscrabble farm. The double-door entry and long halls formed a sanctuary better than the hunchback's cathedral. Tobacco fields, pine-land woods, and endless chores melted away before her books, the school library, history class, and obligatory reports.

During lunch in the stale-smelling cafeteria, seated among the raucous farm boys with their banty-rooster posturing, she felt anxious and different. As often as possible, she sat alone at the Formica tables, away from her classmates. But, when the next grade pushed through clunky doors, the monitor gestured her back to her group.

End-of-the-day bell rang at 3:30 and the school exploded with a rambunctious stampede toward the buses. Stoic drivers stood next to their vehicles while kids climbed aboard. Today, Lee took her time leaving the building, grateful she did not have to endure a packed ride home.

Grace Harris in her '52 Ford sedan waited in the parking lot, two bald tires on the grass and two on the asphalt. The trunk, smashed in when she had backed into a phone pole, was wired closed. A faint patina of dust outlined the once-blue vehicle.

"You-hoo. Over here." Smiling, the woman leaned

from the car window and waved. Lee skipped down the sidewalk and broke into a run. She yanked the door open, slid over the cracked vinyl seat, and gave the woman a kiss on the cheek.

"How was your first day in sixth grade?" Although Grace had a clipped Boston accent, it did not grate on Lee's ears as most northern accents did.

"It was fine. I can check out any book in the library now that I'm in a higher grade. Look. I already got three."

"Well, goodness, I see that you have *Lord of the Flies*."

"It's about school boys turning into savages. Do you think that's possible?"

"Maybe. Under the right circumstances."

"Is it true? Did the plane really crash and leave those boys?"

"Well, no. It's an allegory about how we might treat each other, especially when rules dissolve. I think Golding tried to question our basic natures with this tale."

"My teacher said I should wait to read it until I'm older when I would understand better. What do you think?"

"Oh, I think you're old for your age. Try it. See

if you like it. What else did you get?"

Grace wrestled the car into reverse, maneuvered around, and followed the yellow blobs out in a dust cloud, grinding gears as she shifted. Lee chattered on about her teachers and books.

They drove past the box-shaped post office, across freight train tracks, by the Shell gas station, turned left at the Purina feed store and out of the tired rural community. The car jerked, grunted, and protested with each gear shift.

Shabby farm houses and weed-choked fields edged the blacktop. An overalls-clad farmer, moving his tractor from one field to another, slowed their progress. After a mile, he turned off and the pair rumbled on.

September warmth felt good on Lee's face. She watched Grace's hair twirl in the breeze, catch the light, and flash copper red. Even her freckles sparkled. No matter how often Lee tossed her head, her hair did not dance nor catch the light. Nonetheless, with windows down, she felt carefree and special. She liked being with her mama's friend.

Sand snatched at the wheels and threatened to throw the vehicle into the bar ditch as the pair turned off the paved road onto the dirt track toward the McClarity farm. Dust coiled up in thick ropes and announced their progress.

Grace crunched the gears a last time as she parked under the live oaks at the edge of the hard-pack yard. Pepper, the blue tick hound, set to baying.

Waving from the front stoop, Mama held several galvanized pails. She gave Lee a hug and kissed her on the cheek.

"Good day at school?"

"Yes. I have new library books."

"Good. We'll look at them later. Right now, run change your school things and come help us pick figs." She gave her daughter another peck on the cheek.

"Yes, Mama." Lee jumped onto the plank porch and trotted into the house.

Willowy Grace and Mama, pear shaped with chocolate curls, disappeared around the corner, arm-in-arm.

Lee flew inside her room, flung her dress into a heap on the floor and pulled on jean shorts and a shirt. She bounded outside and grabbed a pail.

The afternoon sun glinted along the lobed leaves and down the hoary bark. Lee smiled and thought how they resembled three twittering birds as their hands darted among the branches picking the plump figs. At these times, for her, the ragged farm receded into a complicated backdrop filled with work and her parents. For the moment, she basked in the closeness of her mother and Grace.

"Honey, go into the barn and see if you can find another pail," Mama said. "These are almost full."

A haven for spiders and rat snakes, the derelict barn smelled of hay and cow manure. Lee took a deep breath, savoring the mingled odors. She rummaged about for a container, poked tentatively under the feed trough, and into the cobwebbed corners.

Stepping back outside, she shaded her eyes against the orange-red sun and hollered. "I can't find anything."

As she watched, her mama brushed a strand of hair from Grace's eyes and tucked it behind her ear. With a slight nod, Grace picked a ripe fig, peeled off the stem and popped it into her friend's mouth. Mama closed her eyes and savored the taste.

Smiling, her mother picked a purple globe, broke it open, and returned the gesture. A single clear drop lingered a moment on Grace's slightly parted lips. She licked it slowly. They stood close, eyes locked on each other.

"Go look in the corn crib." Mama turned in a dreamy movement toward Lee. "There should be something behind the door. Try to find the small tin one." Her voice stopped and hung in the air.

Daddy stood at the corner of the run-down barn, his entire body vibrating, focused on the two women. Greasy bib overalls strained against his belly and thighs. Bushy brows hid dark eyes. Liver-spotted hands opened and closed in fists.

"Girl, they done got enough figs. They ain't needing no more buckets." His voice grated, an untuned fiddle playing off key.

"I think that there red harlot is ready to leave on out. 'Sides, your mama's got evening chores to get done."

Mama's gaze shifted from her husband's face to the doe-soft eyes of her friend. She paused a moment, reached for and gently took the other woman's hand. Despite the softness of her voice, Lee clearly heard her mother.

"Let me put these figs into something else you can take home. I'll walk you to your car. Seems like Henry's a bit irritable this evening." Mama turned and, still holding hands, led Grace away.

Henry glowered at their backs. He scratched his crotch, spit a stream of tobacco juice into the dirt, turned, and stalked toward the tractor shed.

Standing at the gate impatient for the evening milking, Bessie, the orange and white Guernsey cow, lowed mournfully. Summer heat lightning flashed across the west pasture without any hint of rain. The wind rose, rattled dying corn stalks, pushed spent leaves across the yard, and bent grass low.

On Friday, the school bus dropped Lee off at the farm mailbox. Pine trees stood in tin soldier lines beside the sandy track, whispering with every passing breeze. Although she listened hard, she was unable to decipher their murmurings. Lee ambled toward the clapboard house. Jumping up on the rough plank porch, she pulled the screen door open.

"Mama, I'm home."

Silence.

She flopped her school books on the kitchen table and stepped into the narrow hallway.

"I have two new library books. Want to see?"

Again, silence.

Puzzled, Lee turned toward her bedroom and changed into her denim shorts. She wandered out and hung over the back porch rail.

"Mama? Where are you?"

"Yer Mama ain't here. She done gone." Daddy's voice had the gravely whine of a knife on grindstone.

"Gone? Gone where?" Bewildered, Lee stared at his brooding bulk. He stood near the pump house. Sweat beaded on his forehead. Dirt-ringed fingers clenched an ax.

Then it dawned on her. The fig trees were gone. Cut down. Their tri-lobed leaves, delicate globes, and grey limbs lay sprawled in a wrecked mass.

"What happened to the trees? What happened?"

"Never you mind. They was messy. Bothersome. Them trees needed to be cut."

"Why Daddy? Why? Where's Mama?" Lee jumped down the steps and stumbled toward the tangled heap.

"She'll cry over the trees. They were hers. Those were Mama's." Her voice caught in her throat.

65

"Needed to be cut." He turned away.

"Where is she? What's happened?"

"Get on with them evening chores. You got to do the milking til your mama gets herself straight." He stooped and leaned his ax against the pump house corner.

"But what about Mama?"

"Ain't no concern to you, girl. Git on now. I got work to get done. That there old sow be having her pigs soon." Stiffly, he limped toward the farrowing pens. He never looked back.

Lee milked Bessie. Several times, she stopped, propped her head against the cow's side, and cried. Barn cats rubbed against her legs, meowing and begging for a share. Done, but still sniffing, she filled a shallow pan for them and carried the rest into the house.

"Mama? Where are you? What happened?" she murmured.

She wandered from room to room, opened and closed closets, cabinets, and drawers. Tears and snot streamed down her face. She felt dread, black and terrible, settle on her thin shoulders. She wiped her nose on her shirt sleeve.

Outside, she shuffled toward the barns. Stooping over, she stepped into the tiny chicken coop, gathered eggs, and held them in her shirt tail. The hens, already settled on their nighttime roosts, fussed and clucked softly while they jostled for a preferred spot.

"Hurry up with them eggs." Her daddy's voice jarred her. "I'm sending you over to stay with Aunt Josie."

"Why? Where's Mama? What happened?"

"Never mind. Finish up. Git yer school stuff and go on down. Go on before it gets good dark."

Dusk began its descent, dragging muted orange ribbons across the sky. Off in the distance, the lilting call of a screech owl rose over the pines.

Lee stepped out onto the warped grey porch, arms filled with books, clothes stuffed into a paper grocery sack. She closed the door tenderly.

Pepper trotted up the steps to the girl, sat and watched. Lee put the sack down and cradled the animal's face in her hands. His tail thumped a hollow, measured cadence on the weathered wood.

"You got to stay here, Pepper. Aunt Josie's already got dogs. She doesn't want any more."

The girl fondled the hound's long ears, letting them trail through her fingers. Tears pooled in her eyes.

"She doesn't want another girl neither."

Lee stepped off the back stoop. Puffs of powder-fine dust rose about her feet. She stared at the tangled pile in the empty yard.

Three stumps squatted in a line, bleeding sap. She stood a moment, then knelt and stroked the mutilated remnants.

More Than Fruitcake

~~~~~~

At first cold snap, Granny and Granddad, on their way from Atlanta to West Palm Beach for the winter, arrived at our farm. Time to make fruitcakes, a staple and expected Christmas gift. *A Tradition.*

Everyone, including an aunt from down the road and several cousins, gathered around our kitchen table. The day started with hot coffee, or, in the case of me and younger cousins, cups of half milk and half coffee topped off with sugar.

Momma, Aunt Sylvia and Granny did the measuring and mixing. A sixteen-year-old going on thirty cousin started the chopping. Me and another restless eleven-year-old began cracking nuts. Pecan, Brazil and walnut meats surrendered to our probing nimble fingers.

Chartreuse citron, red candied cherries, dark and pale raisins, and sun-browned dates spilled kaleidoscope-like across floured cloths. Sticky fruit, dusted white, tumbled together, transformed into square marbles.

Sunshine streamed through a window, lighting escaped flour clouds. Cinnamon, dark star cloves, and ginger transformed that ordinary farm kitchen into an exotic aromatic country. Scissors clicked, large spoons chimed against bowls, and knives swished across wooden cutting boards creating an orchestral symphony of preparation.

Aunt Sylvia, who pulled her hair straight back into a hard little bun at the nape of her neck, usually started it – *'it'* being the latest community news. Her round face glowed and her hands flew about when she talked. In fact, she spoke with more animation than all the other Jefferson women put together. Some folks called her dramatic.

"Well, Bethany and Charlie were at it again. Sheriff Moore had to drive all the way out to their farm Saturday night. By the time he got to the house, Bethany's eye had swollen shut." Aunt Sylvia wiped her hands across a damp dish towel.

"'Course, Charlie denied even touching her, much less hitting her. Talk has it though, he smelled of whiskey real bad."

"I heard Sheriff finally gave up trying to talk reason and drove back to town. Left them right there." Tight lines around Granny's old eyes betrayed her anger.

"Now, I know Sheriff thinks stuff like that's a private family matter," Aunt Sylvia barged in, "but he did say he'd haul Charlie in if Bethany pressed charges. What with him being drunk and beating her. Why on earth that woman won't leave him, I don't know. It's beyond me."

Granny, usually described as ponderous, gritted her teeth. "It scares those kids to death when he gets to hitting and cussing. That oldest one, John Lee, might jump in one day. He's as tall as Charlie now. You know he feels protective about his mother. What with him having a different daddy and all."

"Y'all remember now, everything is a tradeoff." Momma, a family beauty with her chestnut hair, often disarmed the most acid tongue with simple insight. "That man provides good for the family when he's working. Furthermore, his handsome good looks and sweet-talking ways have bolstered Bethany. She's always thought of herself as not good enough since she never graduated high school, was divorced, and had all those kids. When he picked her out, she felt special. I'm not excusing his actions, God love him, but trouble only starts when he gets into the bottle."

"Yeah. And, he uses those charming ways to his utmost advantage." Aunt Sylvia wiped spilled flour off the table. "I know and you know, if something happened to him, Bethany and those six kids would struggle hard. *Real* hard." She cocked an eyebrow and nodded.

"They might be better off without him," said Granny. Her lips tightened into a hard, thin line. She shook her head. "He's got a dark mean streak. I still think Bethany ought to get shed of him."

"God knows but she's got her hands full with those twin babies as it is," Momma said in her slow, rich drawl. "She's smart. Why, just look at the way she's raising those children and dealing with him. If she can handle things on the little dab of money he gives her to run the house, she can manage anything."

Talk droned on. Me and my cousins kept our heads down and hands busy. We tried to appear absorbed in cracking nuts and chopping, and not in eavesdropping on grown-up talk. Pecans shelled, we shifted to Brazil nuts and walnuts. Momma made her cakes with lots of nuts for crunch. She said they added texture against the soft and sweet candied fruits.

"By the way, did you hear about Glenda Sloan? They put her in the Waycross hospital last week." Aunt Sylvia never simply worked. She talked, no matter what went on around her. "Seems that nervous stomach problem cropped up again. Probably an ulcer and she'll most likely stay another week."

We didn't see much of the Sloan family because they attended the Millwood Primitive Baptist Church. But, since they bought groceries at Winn-Dixie, same as us, we considered them neighbors.

"How's he doing with Glenda in the hospital?" Momma said. "Do we need to take meals by for him?"

"Their married daughter's already taking her daddy and those boys over meals." Aunt Sylvia paused a moment and looked up through her thick glasses. "But you know him. He won't even heat water. Lord help us, but that man's worthless when it comes to taking care of himself. Those boys aren't any better."

"This is *not* the first time she's been in with stomach trouble." Granny raised her eyebrows, flounced over to the sink, and washed sticky goo off her hands. "That old man worries her to death. Pastor needs to visit and get the church ladies involved. That'll please her and set him to fuming." She chuckled at the thought.

Old man Sloan farmed tobacco and hogs a few miles from us. Known to be cantankerous and rough on his wife, he was nonetheless considered a hard-working farmer. Community women always pitched in and helped the married daughter keep the house up and old man Sloan fed until Glenda got through her stomach trouble and back on her feet.

Chopping, flouring, and talk rattled on. I listened real close and watched while Momma measured out home-churned butter, flour, and cracked yard eggs, separating whites from yolks. Her hands, considered large for a woman, creamed the batter smooth.

"Well, talk has it that Smith woman got caught at the Red Rooster Diner picking up a trucker from out toward Pierce County." Aunt Sylvia talked as she greased several tube pans and four loaf-sized ones. "That caused quite a set to. Her husband's fit to be tied. Talk is he might move them off somewhere along the Florida panhandle. Get a new start."

Momma glanced up. "Well, she sings in the Methodist Church choir and has a beautiful voice. Her man helps clean up church grounds, make repairs, and usher on Sundays. All said and done, they are good people, even if a little peculiar."

Ignoring the comment, Granny barged in. "That woman runs around with anything in pants. Can't figure out how her and him got together in the first place. Good Lord knows he's boring as a fence post."

By the time everything got measured and folded in, those women had discussed the latest community gossip and news while Momma filled the pans with rich, chunky batter. She wiped her hands and dabbed her fingers in a bit of Crisco. She lightly dipped candied pineapple rings, cherry halves, and blanched almonds in Karo syrup, arranging them like flowers on top. Each cake was transformed into a baker's work of art.

With everything in the oven, Granny poured herself another cup of coffee. She took it black, no sugar. "Did you hear tell Clyde Williams went and got a job at the pulpwood mill over to Valdosta?"

Aunt Sylvia poured herself coffee, stirred in cream and watched the color change. "That's a long drive every day. He probably won't last." She sipped noisily from her cup. "I know Bea can use the money, while it's coming. With hog prices low, they need something besides the farm. That man don't like to do anything except fool with them hounds. Good thing she has her grocery job at Safeway."

"Well, you know, not many women around here work outside the house. She might look like a country bumpkin, but she's a tenacious spirit with an unconventional heart." Momma smiled and looked out the window. "Her homemade flour-sack dresses are a camouflage, if you ask me. I think she's modern and independent. She can take care of herself without Clyde."

Granny stood up and refilled her coffee. "You girls wash up these bowls and stuff, then go on outside."

Freed, we scooted out to poke around the corn crib for snakes, climb in the fig trees, and dig through the hay stacks.

Being young may come with problems but, then again, being grown-up did too. Seemed to me it didn't get better, only more complicated. I pondered on shared work, farm chores, and our little community.

By late afternoon, we staggered back into the house, a bit intoxicated with all the goings-on. Cakes, fresh from the oven, sat cooling in neat rows along knife-scarred counter tops. Granny pulled down jars of homemade peach brandy and lightly drizzled the cakes before wrapping them in liquor-soaked cloths. Placed in huge lard tins, they would season for months, flavors mingling and mellowing. Pungent odors, so strong I tasted them, lingered in the kitchen until after dark.

At the Christmas holidays, the moist, seasoned cakes reappeared and were mailed to distant relatives, served at church get-togethers, or donated to our school holiday bazaar.

The years unreeled and always Granny, Momma, and Aunt Sylvia gathered to make the traditional fruitcakes. I graduated high school, moved to a bigger city and attempted to shake off any farm dust. My cousins married. Some stayed around South Georgia. Some moved up to Atlanta. Others relocated to Mississippi. Occasionally they came back with their new husbands and babies, always claiming they'd come to help, but really showing off.

Talk ranged over who in the family or among the neighbors lost a job, married, divorced or had another baby. Who was sick and needed help, who missed Sunday church a little too regular, and what to bring for the next homecoming dinner-on-the-ground. A litany of who died and how the funeral went got recited. Even when told earlier, family and community events were nonetheless discussed again during the annual baking.

By the late 1980s, new families moved in, several factories opened up, and business boomed across the county. The high school finally integrated. Farms sold to big producers. The Red Rooster Diner burned down one night during a summer lightning storm. Arson was suspected, but no one ever proved it.

Momma called me with the news that old man Sloan's tractor slipped in a sink hole and rolled on him while plowing one Wednesday. His wife Glenda moved in with her married daughter after he died. I heard she never did have any more stomach trouble. Sheriff retired and his deputy got elected.

Bethany and Charlie were still together, a puzzle

to me especially since she'd gotten her brood up and off on their own. No need for her to stay with him. The twins moved to Louisiana and married some real nice girls. The two middle youngsters went as far as North Carolina, found jobs, and started families. The oldest girl graduated from community college and moved to Jacksonville. She never married. John Lee never married neither. He moved to Waycross, a neighboring town, to be around if his mother needed him.

Momma told me that, with everyone gone, Bethany earned her GED and started nurse training. She waited tables and earned her own school money. County hospital hired her as soon as she got her RN.

Charlie kept drinking. His good looks faded and charm wore down thin. He showed up late for work or else never showed up at all. Drifted from job to job, got fired from near every mill and factory in our three-county area. They lived on what she made as a nurse.

One morning he got up, made coffee and waited for Bethany to come home from night shift. Shot her dead as soon as she walked in the door.

He called the county law, crumpled down at

the table, and waited. Bethany still had on her nurse uniform.

By the time Sheriff arrived the bright red blood splattered across her uniform had turned black. Sheriff said the coffee was untouched and cold. Like Bethany.

Aunt Sylvia told me about it during a visit home after the funeral. She said Sheriff brought Charlie handcuffed to the grave after everyone left. The children didn't want him there during the service. This time, while Aunt Sylvia talked, she gripped her coffee cup real hard until her knuckles turned white.

Granny Jones took off her glasses, sat silent, and stared out the window. Squirrels chattered and raced up the oaks. Somewhere a woodpecker drummed out a tat-tat, looking for insects.

"I guess there are different kinds of needs." Momma's voice got soft. "Those two were bound by rough times. Hard to say if they stayed married out of love or need or helplessness. For certain, the children grew closer to their mother and each other out of those hardships. They certainly took the bitter and sweet together."

Bethany had finally left Charlie, but not the

way I expected.

By autumn, with corn stalks rustling in the fields, Granddad passed and Granny relocated to a daughter's house in Alabama. Aunt Sylvia left for Baton Rouge where it was warmer. Bea moved into town and got promoted from cashier to fresh produce manager. Her man Clyde stayed with his hounds in the country. Somewhere along the line, he simply faded away.

After Momma died and Daddy sold the farm, I didn't go back home. Over time, I lost touch. I lived different places, mostly in the South, except for a few years in California.

Sometimes I feel an autumn chill and remember the sound of dry corn fields rattling. Or a door slams, and I see a torn screen banging against a pine frame. Occasionally, an oak groans as I walk past, and I feel a terrible burden of years pulling against time.

I don't make fruitcake any more. Still, when the holidays roll around, the sight of those cakes displayed at Walmart makes me think of my home town and that gathering of women. Quietly, I mail order my holiday gourmet treat from the Collin Street Bakery down in Texas or from Abbey monks at a Missouri monastery.

As winter grows deep and Christmas arrives, I cut a thick slice, pour a cup of coffee, and gaze out the window, remembering real, homemade fruit-cake. I savor those spice-laced memories of joy and hard times spiked with a bite of whiskey.

City friends tease me about fruitcake, ridiculing its odd texture and taste. I nod, smile and say, "It's more than fruitcake. It's memories. It's *Tradition*."

Last Love

~~~~~~

Leroy Jackson moved his ponderous frame toward the table under moss-draped oaks. He had a pronounced limp in his right leg, wore greasy bib overalls, and led a hound on a frayed rope.

"Y'all men give me one of them there sign-up forms." He pointed and drawled in a demanding tone. His left cheek bulged with chewing tobacco and brown drool seeped into the creases around his mouth. He didn't wipe.

"Hello, Leroy." One of the men behind the table glanced up. "That Queenie you got with you? Need one form do you?"

Leroy grunted. He took the registration paper with grimy, gnarled fingers and laboriously filled in blanks, stopping often to lick his pencil stub. He did not bother to step away from the table, causing men behind to shuffle around his bulk for their forms.

The hound sat at his feet, yawned, then stretched out, head on her paws. Her russet coat, common to Redbones, mirrored autumn light. She sported two white toes on one foot and a small patch on her chest.

Sun dripped through tree branches in shades of umber and orange and pooled among leaves. Parked askew in the oak grove, cars and trucks marked spots where folks set up their camps. At dark, a bonfire would summon bluegrass fiddlers, hunters, and spectators to officially start the week-long competition.

Leroy, locally known as a bootlegger and ne'er-do-well, carried a stench of meanness about him. He had been married three times to straight-laced, good Christian women, each who left in turn, either by running off or dying. He never seemed to notice or be bothered by the manner of their leaving. One thing for certain though, he loved hunting and was unashamedly proud of his hounds.

At seventy-four, he aimed to win the Ozark Hills and Hollows Coon Dog Hunt Contest with

Queenie, his sole remaining hound. A last great endeavor.

Leroy handed his form to the same fellow behind the table.

"Well, you know the rules," the man said, accepting the paper. "You draw numbers for your night, go out with whoever draws with you, and judge follows. Y'all bring in all the coons you can get before sunup. Judge scores on which hound strikes, barks up first, stays treed, and your tag count."

Again, Leroy grunted. Great bushy eyebrows hid his eyes. He mostly lived outdoors, so had a craggy look that harsh weather pounds into a face.

Moving off toward the campground edge, he sat under a pine tree, flopped his gunny sack nearby, and carefully laid his rifle across it. He ate cold biscuits and fried fatback, which he shared with his dog, and drank deeply from his crock jug knowing it'd be only a few short hours before evening drawing.

Leroy stretched out on a ragged quilt. Queenie curled beside him. He laid a callused hand on her head and softly scratched around her ears, the only gentleness he allowed himself to show, provided no one was near.

He slept through bonfire lighting, pre-hunt bragging and banjo picking. He woke with a start as folks gathered for the drawing. Struggling, he pulled himself to standing against the tree trunk, and hobbled stiffly toward the firelight. Orange-red sparks floated into a night sky. Pungent smells of wood smoke and pine knots wafted over the crowd.

"Now, men," said a hunt monitor, "we draw numbers. Whatever your number, that's the night you go out. Single entries get paired up by drawing. Four teams go out separately each night with a judge, in different directions, on opposite sides of the river. Everybody needs to take their own lights and guns."

Numbers got drawn and men shuffled around. Leroy drew a three; he'd go out Wednesday night with Paul Irving from near Pineville, Missouri. At fourteen, Paul relished hunting.

His ma had named him after the biblical Paul, saying that no matter where he traveled he'd help folks along the way. His grandpa, a renowned hound breeder, taught him hunting.

Weighing less than forty pounds, Paul's clay-colored hound, Daisy Mae, appeared almost dainty.

Smallest in a litter of eleven, she never sold. Grandpa didn't want to knock her in the head as culls often were. Instead, he gave her to Paul, telling him to make what he could out of her.

"Gawd damn whelp of a kid," Leroy roared. "I ain't come all this here way to hunt with no runt dog and a still-wet young'un." He stalked toward the officials, pushed his huge belly forward, and bellowed in a hard, grating voice.

"Draw again. I ain't huntin' with them two. Queenie's a coon hound, not no durn training dog. I ain't gonna stand for this."

"You know the rules," a monitor said. "Doesn't matter who a hound goes out with, judge's decision goes to the first one to strike, move out on a track, bark up, stay treed until called off, and number of coon tags. Go with who you drew or quit the contest. Up to you."

The officials stared at Leroy, faces blank. The crowd shuffled about a little but stood silent.

"Y'all ought not to let kids in this thing. They ain't earned no rights." He flung a murderous look at those gathered around and stomped off, black with rage.

On Wednesday, wind picked up and took on a

frigid edge. Metal-gray storm clouds roiled over-head as daylight gave up and dark descended.

When Leroy and Queenie with Paul and Daisy stepped up to start, the crowd fell silent, waiting to see if he would create another fuss. He did not. Deliberately though, he shoved past Paul, crowd-ing him and Daisy Mae into stepping back.

Reeve Davis, an Arkansas man, got assigned as their judge.

"Leroy you've done this before and you know the rules. Paul, this is your first big competition. Just keep in mind the things your grandpa taught you. Trust your hound and let her do the hunting. I'll keep the score."

Reeve looked off into the dark. "Cold ground holds scent pretty good, but this wind scatters it. That means hounds have to work harder. Let's get moving."

The three men with the two hounds walked to-ward the grey river. Spectators clustered together and followed to the bank, but went no further.

Leroy unleashed Queenie ahead of Paul and stalked off west along the bank, not looking back.

Daisy ran to Queenie as soon as set loose, and jumped about, face-licking and whining. Queenie tolerated the attention for a few minutes then settled down, nose to ground, tail flagging as she worked.

Several hundred yards down river, she opened, bawling her excitement as she charged through underbrush. Daisy honored, running close behind. Judge, Leroy, and Paul listened, and then trailed hound music to a dried cornfield, not far from the river.

Leroy fell behind in trappy undergrowth, struggled to keep up, and paused frequently to catch his breath. He felt his gimp leg throbbing and cursed his pain in a low growl.

Reeve Davis and Paul hurried ahead, keeping as close to the hounds as possible. Queenie's bawl deepened and grew aggressive. Daisy's chop played under-chords.

At a lone hickory tree, a third of the way into the cornfield, Reeve and Paul found the hounds barking up, moaning, teeth clicking. They stood and watched, then moved forward, shining lights into leafless branches.

"We need to wait on Leroy." The judge looked back across the field. "I think corn stubble is holding him up."

Both stood still and watched baying hounds, front feet planted on the hickory trunk, bark up.

Finally, Leroy stumbled in, breathing hard and unable to talk. Reeve acknowledged the older man with a nod and turned.

"Paul, you take the shot. Queenie was strike hound. Both hounds stayed treed." Reeve wrote his decision in his notebook.

The boy chambered a shell, aimed, and dropped the coon clean.

"Dead coon." Paul praised Daisy with a release command. "Good hound. Good hound. Dead coon."

Queenie hesitated, backed off, whined and looked at Leroy. He limped over to the dead coon, nudged it with his boot and released her with "Good girl. Dead coon. Dead."

With hounds leashed, the group moved down a deep narrow hollow and across a bench parallel to the river. As soon as set loose, both dogs ran shoulder to shoulder, and scoured north through brush before they dropped off a dirt bank into heavy thickets. Music signaled another track running down and across a ridgeline.

This time, having to climb up before sliding down, Leroy's great weight, poor balance, and gimp leg caused him to move even slower.

Judge and Paul arrived first. Two half-grown coons peered down from an oak tree. Leroy stumbled up several minutes later.

"Queenie got strike points. Daisy treed. Both hounds stayed." Reeve held his light high to catch reflection in the raccoons' eyes.

"You want the shot or should Paul take it again?" he said to the old man.

"I'm gonna take it." Despite a cold wind, Leroy sweated. Breathing hard, he cocked his rifle and fired. A clean miss.

"Damn," he said. He chambered a second shell and managed to shoot the highest coon. He botched a third shot. The coon dropped drunkenly, bounced off a limb, and attempted to crawl away. Queenie lunged forward and, with a clean neck snap, killed the wounded animal.

"I ain't in habit missing a shot. Huntin' with some fool little dog done throw'd me off." Leroy bent down to stroke Queenie's head as if apologizing to her.

Paul stood quietly with his hand on Daisy.

"Mr. Leroy, I'm sorry you don't like me and Daisy, but she's a good hound." Paul glanced down at Daisy and bent to attach his rope. "My grandpa gave her to me. He taught me hunting. He told me 'trust the hound.' I'm gonna do that."

Reeve smiled and nodded agreement. "Looks to me like they make a fine pair working off each other. They got three coons and both have points."

Leroy snorted. "Got no need for some half-growed peckerwood and a runt cull." He twisted on his heel and limped toward the river.

Judge shrugged and followed while Paul and Daisy Mae trailed behind.

Wind moaned, light drizzle turned to rain, and night shadows grew thick. At two o'clock, six hours before sun-up, there was plenty of time for another cast. The trio walked the slippery river bottom. Willow and birch crowded the bank, dragging sweeper fingers in the water. Small sand bars here and there offered prime coon forage sites.

Unleashed, both hounds immediately opened. Scent, hot enough to make them scream, drew them under weeping trees, back and forth, back and forth. They scoured river's edge until Queenie let loose one long howl and jumped into the water. She swam for a gravel bar.

The men, following along the bank, stumbled

over vines and dead limbs. Leroy tripped, dropped
his light and fell hard on his shoulder.

"Damn dark. Can't see nuthin," he said pushing
himself to standing. Mud sucked at his boots and,
with no light, he slowed even further.

Hound music grew sweet then descended into a
snarling fracas. Queenie found a boar coon feeding
on a sandbar and grabbed it by the haunch. The
ringtail whipped around and seized her in a death
grip. Entwined in a slobbering ball of blood and
hair, the two animals struggled.

Following the older hound, Daisy pulled herself up on the bar precisely as the old bull broke
loose from Queenie. He scurried toward a swirling
side channel.

Shaking her head, Queenie splattered blood on
nearby rocks, paused a moment baying, and leapt
into water only steps behind the veteran boar.

With his grizzled snout slightly above water,
bull coon swam for the opposite channel. Luring
Queenie into a fast current next to him, he turned
and climbed cat-like on her head. His size forced
her under while he rode above water.

Each time the hound's head broke surface, the
ringtail shifted his weight, biting, scratching, and

driving her under again and again.

Waist high in river water, men squinted and watched the dark silhouettes in their grim contest.

"I can't shoot the sumbitch." An impotent rage strangled Leroy. "I can't shoot. I'm likely to hit Queenie."

He stumbled against rocks hidden under water and fell hard. He sank, sputtered, and gagged as his weight and wet overalls dragged at him.

Reeve dropped his light, ducked forward, grabbed Leroy and yanked him toward the bank. Paul waded out, looped his hand around a strap and pulled with all his young strength.

"Get my hound." Leroy railed helplessly. "Gawd damn it all to hell, get my hound. Leave me be."

The trio, floundering, tripped into a deadfall at river bend. Entangled in tree branches, they grunted and groped against each other, arms flailing. Reeve held on to the older man and heaved him toward solid footing.

"Boy, get the lights. We got to see where we going," shouted Reeve.

Paul fumbled, found two lights and pounded them against the heel of his hand. Still waterlogged, they flickered weakly.

"Get my hound. Get my hound." Leroy coughed. His legs gave way and he collapsed across a downed tree. He thrashed uselessly, fighting river current, darkness, and creeping cold.

"Get my Queenie. Leave me be. Gawd damn it. Get my hound. Don't let that boar drown her."

Daisy, exhausted from her struggle, plunged back into the river and swam toward the hunted and hunter in their watery struggle. With a lurch, she grabbed the tough old bull by his tail.

Snarling, he jumped off Queenie's head and paddled toward a dead tree partially laying up a gravel bank. The young hound, towed by the coon, hung on. He heaved himself out of water and twisted around into Daisy's face. She yelped, loosened her grip, and was swept downstream.

Queenie, free of her adversary's weight, paddled across the whitewater current. Rain grew heavy and pounding. Hell's own blackness shrouded the contestants.

Reeve held Leroy's head above water. He part shoved, part hauled the heavy man up the embankment, yelling at Paul.

"Get the hounds. You got to get them before rain brings the river up. I can manage this feller."

Paul waded back into the current screaming.

"Daisy! Get to. Get to. Here. Here." A frantic edge crept into his voice. "Come girl. Come Daisy."

Hounds whined and paced up and down along a gravel bar under a steep bank. Finally, Daisy, then Queenie, jumped into fast water and swam toward Paul. He waded out as far as possible, waited for them, grabbed each by their collar, and slopped toward higher ground.

Heavy fog floated low over the river and daylight reflected off white sycamores before Reeve could summon help from hunt officials and get Leroy trucked out.

Paul hiked back with both hounds, stopping occasionally to pet their bloodstained faces. Without the weight of lanterns and guns, he made good time. Once back at camp, he kept an arm slung around both she-dogs, hugging one on either side of him.

Reeve went out several nights helping to judge final contestants. Two brothers from Mississippi won on Friday.

Leroy had several busted ribs, a broken hand and a wrenched knee. Worse, he caught pneumonia. Since he'd run off his latest woman and even his grown children, he found himself alone. Queenie got tethered in his dilapidated barn. Although he hobbled out each evening to feed her, he was guilt-ridden at keeping her tied, unable to roam and hunt.

Paul took Daisy home to his mother, an experienced hand at sewing up critters. Within the week, the pair roamed about hunting squirrels during daylight and coons at night.

One afternoon, a good year later, Paul looked up as Leroy's pickup rattled toward the house. A hound box bounced around in back. Daisy rushed out from under porch steps to bark and announce the arrival. Paul stepped off the front stoop. His ma stood in the entrance way, one hand on the screen door and the other shading her eyes.

Leroy parked under an oak at the yard's edge. Sticking an arm out the truck window, he fumbled for the door handle. He half-slid and half-fell out of the cab, gimped along the running board, and propped his great frame against the front wheel well.

"I come here 'bout my hound," he announced.

Breathing hard, he stood a moment, and pulled himself along the truck side to the rear. He fumbled with the tailgate before finally letting it crash down on the bumper. With stiff, knotty fingers, he opened the hound box.

Queenie sashayed out, tail wagging, licking at him.

Daisy sat on her haunches, nose pointed up, and cut loose with a long howl. Paul walked into the yard, eyes wide. Ma stepped out on her sagging porch, watchful, still shading her eyes.

Leroy stared off into woods and fields that surrounded the weather-beaten, clapboard house, listening to bird calls and squirrel chatter. He remained silent a long time.

"I can't get 'round much no more 'cause this here crippled leg. Can't clean my gun good nor take care Queenie 'cause my hands." His voice rough, he hawked up phlegm, bent over, and spat.

"These ribs ain't healed right and I still got this here cough. Truth be told, I can't walk them woods like I done."

He reached into his pocket, pulled out a chunk of Bull Durham and bit off a plug. Brown tobacco juice oozed out of the corner of his mouth and down his chin as he chewed.

At the edge of the cornfield, a crow cawed and pumped up and down on a fence post.

"Ain't no life for a huntin dog, be tied up all the time. They gotta be out. They gotta hunt. It's they nature." He paused, spit a viscous stream into the dust, and took a deep breath. He let it out, slow and ragged.

"I'm gonna give Queenie to you. You hunt her. You and that there little runt hound. They a good pair."

He stroked Queenie's head, petting around her ears and down her neck. She sat at his feet, tail thumping, and watched his face.

"I never could rightly tolerate them women I married. Didn't care for none of them young'uns we had neither. But I do care for this here hound."

His hand lingered on her head, then dropped against his grease-stained overalls. He clenched his jaw, pivoted back to the truck cab, climbed in, slammed the door, and rattled off. A rooster-tail of dust and grit marked his going.

Queenie gave out with one long, mournful note which carried across the cornfield and into the tree line. She sat, looked down the road until the dust settled, then turned, and trotted off. The little hound followed.

The Stooper

~~~~~~

N o sound's as sweet as that ear-splitting, nerve-grating bell when horses break from the starting gate. Nothing compares to the surge of power, pounding roll of hooves, flashing colored silks, and jocks perched high on a horse's withers.

I played the ponies a little, sometimes won, sometimes didn't. No matter. I didn't go for betting. I hung at the track for the horses.

Watching those athletic animals made the hair on the back of my neck prickle and goose bumps cover my arms. Rain, shine, or cold, my days—as often as possible—uncoiled at the track with its great dirt oval, shed row backside, greasy canteen, and betting windows peopled by crippled souls living on myopic dreams.

Years back, as a young woman, I'd left home, looking for something besides life on a hard-scrabble tobacco farm. Not sure quite how, but I eventually ended up in Hot Springs. Time I arrived, town was decades past prohibition and its heyday as a gangster vacation spot. Then and now, Oaklawn Park housed the only parimutuel Thoroughbred betting in Arkansas. I fell hopelessly under the spell of track life.

Didn't make any money. Instead, I found freak-ish winters, sodden summers, seedy high rollers, and a nefarious backside empire. Everyone worked cheap and harbored a hidden demon.

Women, especially my kind, got hired after white farm boys and nut-colored immigrants. I took what I could get, usually green or rank horses, tedious grooming jobs, hot walking, and shed row work. The leftovers of the horse world. No classy gym for me. Mucking stalls, wrapping legs, soaping tack, and hauling feed gave me all the squat, bend and lift I needed to stay thin.

After a time, trainers got used to seeing me around, liked my work and the way I handled the ponies. When a regular exercise ride didn't show, I'd get the breeze. Unofficial and on the side, of course. And, less money.

My first time to sling a leg over a thousand pounds of raw adolescent power gave me an adrenaline rush like nothing I'd had before or since.

One leggy bay, Red Romero, stole my heart. I groomed and wrapped him a few seasons. Licensed riders breezed him. Apprentice jocks or broke-down old timers usually took the ride. He stayed in the money for a while, but gradually slipped back until he got left at the starting gate. Bowed tendons, popped splints, and close to seven years old, he raced on courage and bone for a spell.

I stayed with him long as I could, even when his trainer didn't pay. Last I saw of Red, he shipped to dirt-track claiming races in Oklahoma. Places where stewards turned a blind eye and owners didn't question how a horse got to the winner's circle.

I cried over that one.

Still, for a gal, I did pretty good. Got started on my license and worked up to breezing, although I never got beyond end-of-the-road trainers in class. Grooming and mucking backside helped me make ends meet.

When I turned forty-five, it all caught up with

me. Hard spills, unruly horses, endless hours, bad weather, and trainers slow in paying caused me to reconsider my one-way career choice. Stopped cold turkey. Gave up shed row work, grooming, breezing, and all my prayers for any license.

I hired on at a plant in Little Rock and worked a late-afternoon-to-midnight shift. During racing season, I'd get off and share the road with long-haul truckers driving Interstate 30 to Hot Springs, radio tuned to an all-night jazz station to smooth the way. On the edge of town, I'd stop by a round-the-clock diner for an order of grits, two eggs over easy, and sweet black coffee.

Afterwards, I'd point my rust-tinted pickup toward the track about the time dawn opened her sleepy eyes. I'd lean against the rail and watch as exercise riders breezed horses that snorted in rhythm. Hopefuls would be out galloping, testing their speed and matching each other stride-for-stride toward some future glory. Youngsters, ponied down the backside, got started on track lessons while they built strength. If I ever had a religion, this was it.

That's how I met Lester Groh. First time I saw him, I still worked backside. He hawked programs at the south entrance for a dollar. Only he was not part of any authorized track personnel. He picked up used programs from discouraged bettors and resold them by undercutting new program prices.

He wore a frayed army jacket with a 1st Air Cav horsehead patch. Under his knit hat, Lester's face had the dirty texture of cracked shoe leather. His blond hair hung in thick strings to his shoulders. You know, honky dreadlocks. Truth be told, it resembled an abandoned rat's nest. He walked crooked, one leg bent and shorter than the other.

And, he coughed. Deep from the chest. Late in the day when his 'medicine' wore off, Lester ranted. Sometimes track security tossed him out as one more disposable Nam vet unable to cope. Not often, but occasionally, someone besides me ran interference for him.

As day ended, people drifted out, tossing away betting slips. Sometimes they discarded one, walked off, and zoned on to something else just as stewards settled a challenge. Most often, a person simply got oiled and dropped a ticket.

That's where Lester came in. He'd bend down and pick up those stubs. A confirmed track stooper, he even got out in what the day-job crowd called bad weather.

"How ya' doing, Alice?" Lester greeted me. He seemed to look beyond my less-than-feminine appearance. I felt he saw *me*. Saw my short brown hair, scarred hands, flat chest, and nondescript clothes.

"What's the pick today?" I said, fishing in my pocket for a bill.

"Take 4 horse in the fifth." He took my bill and handed me a used *Daily Racing Form*.

"The 4 horse?" I skimmed down the Form. "Pocket the Sweets? Looks like a sleeper with no sheet. She even broke her maiden?"

"Got Hot Pockets on the bottom line. I know that breeding. Besides, today is the day."

"Today?" I cocked an eyebrow and searched his face. "Got anything else?"

"Play across the board with 8 and 6 horses."

"Across the board?"

"That's right." His face was blank. "Do what I say. Otherwise, why ask?"

Something about Lester's voice and his piercing glare to bet Sweets struck a chord. Never hurt to lay a few bucks on an insider tip. What did it matter?

"You got something you want to put down?"

"Yeah. Put this with your bet." He handed me several crumpled, dirty fins. "I ain't here when you get done, give it to that wetback cleaning woman. You know, one takes care of the toilets."

"You a saint for Mexicans in your old age now?"

"No. She treats me like a person. That's all."

He limped toward the turnstile. I hurried on for the betting window and a caffeine fix.

Cup in hand, I studied the program. Number 4 horse was a three-year old mare by Sweet William out of Hot Pockets. Listed as Pocket the Sweets with Eddie Chavez in the irons and Mutt Smith down as trainer and owner. A claiming race. On paper, Sweets had the power to win.

I strolled over to backside, gave a polite nod to Wilbur, the ancient Negro gate keeper, and stepped again into a nether world of dreams and altered horses running with someone's last dime and dying hope.

Morning mist hung low across paddocks. A light frost blanketed the grounds and thin spirals of steam rose from manure piles. Bright-eyed horses looked over stall half-doors and snorted great explosions of breath, visible for fleeting seconds before evaporating into a grey morning.

"Well, if it ain't *Mr.* Alice. How you doing, gal?"

Mutt had a vinegary disposition and, when he spoke, his voice spilled out of a dark mouth-hole. He clutched a half-smoked cigar between his teeth.

"Want to wrap a nag?" He leered at me. "Can't nobody do it like a broad." A smirk played across his face.

"Nope. Don't do horses anymore."

"You still do women?"

"That's none of your business."

Slowly he removed the soppy butt from his mouth and squinted at me. He opened his jacket and pushed his belly out. Shirt buttons strained against his flesh.

"Not wrappin'? Then what the hell you doin' back here? Don't need some butch trash gettin' in the way, spookin' my horses."

"Mutt, you got nothing but broke down nags. Only energy they got is what you inject."

"Watch that mouth, lesbo." He spat and glared at me. "That don't answer what you doin' back here if you not lookin' to work."

"I came to see Sweets. Program says you're running her in the fifth."

He glared at me, grunted, deliberately turned

his back, and stalked off. I stood a minute and watched him.

Down the row, a groom slipped an exercise saddle off a tall chestnut finished with a workout. Horse lowered his head for the halter and the pair turned toward a wash stand. Sweat and saddle marks melted as water splashed against his copper-red coat. The colt shook himself. Droplets jumped into the air, hung in a bright halo and disappeared in the time it took to draw a breath.

A little farther down, the sharp tapping noise of a farrier's hammer vibrated. In the distance, a dog barked. Veterinarians, eyes narrowed, moved in medicinal-smelling whispers from horse to horse. The green odor of alfalfa and horse musk floated in the air.

I moseyed on toward Sweets's stall. She looked out over a half-door and whuffed at me. I knew mares didn't usually stay on competitive tracks long. They run in the money and retire to breeding, slide down in class, or get sent to the killers. For some reason, Mutt kept Sweets on.

I looked her over. She had a finely-chiseled head, a white snip on her nose, a long neck, and lean black body. Although a tad short in the back, there was good depth in her hindquarters, and a nice slope to her shoulder. Breeding said she could run. I opened the stall door and rubbed her legs. Tight, no heat. She stood relaxed and curious, nuzzled my shoulder a couple of times, and turned back to her hay net.

I caught Lester again at the backside kitchen. Cook or waitress generally ran him out, but at this hour they got busy changing from breakfast grill to burgers, so didn't bother.

"What's the story on that filly?"

"Mutt held her back. Told jock to keep her on edge of the money. Let'er slide down in class, run her in a claiming race, and take the whole damn thing. Purse isn't much, but odds will be up there."

"Today's the day?" I picked up a large cup and filled it with brew. "How did you come by this information?"

"Feller owes me." He glared around the room. "I pick up more than stubs."

"You get paid with a long shot tip? Odds are 50-1 on her. He must owe you big time."

"He does." Lester nodded. "Put a dime on her if you got it. Build your retirement fund. Consider it my Christmas present."

"Why me?"

"You're an ugly dyke, but I like you. You handle nags with respect. Besides, someone's got to buy my joe."

A missing tooth gave his face an unbalanced, deranged look. He clenched his jaw as he turned, rubbed his bum leg, and hobbled through the greasy canteen. I paid for two coffees, threw in a heaping spoon of sugar, and hurried out.

A person could get hurt passing along tips like this. I also knew that, generally speaking, city cops don't have time to investigate track derelicts, John Q Public never notices hangers-on at the gate, and race officials would sigh "good riddance" at one less stooper. Backside workers, however, would understand the lesson.

When the gate opened for the fifth race, things unreeled in slow motion. Sweets had the ten hole, a lot of ground to cover to get to the rail. She dug in, nosed her way to the middle of the pack, and settled into stride. At the club house turn, jockey laid his stick *hard* across her rump. She exploded. Those long legs reached out and grabbed great chunks of real estate. Running low, ears back, she waved her black tail in every face all the way to the wire. Galloped two lengths ahead of the field. I held my ticket and smiled when tote board flashed 4.

I didn't hear Lester come up until his phlegmy cough splattered into my consciousness. He hawked and spat before he thrust a grimy hand with several smudged tickets toward me.

"Cash these. Got'em at the bar. Folks tossed live ones along with others."

I took the stubs, sorted through them, and nodded.

"What shall I do with the money?"

"I done told you. Give it to that spic." His voice vibrated with a hard edge.

"Don't you want it? For your medicine? You sound bad."

"No." He coughed again, a deep, chest-splitting hack. "You know good as I do, hustle like this only works one time."

He stumbled off, stopped, and bent over coughing. Spat again, stood upright, wiped his mouth across his jacket sleeve, and limped on.

Lights flicked through approaching dusk as the gate clanged open on the day's last race. January cold crept along rails. Fans blew on gloveless fingers and hurried inside to place final bets.

Forecast called for another hard freeze.

By morning, heavy frost crunched under foot. Thin, transparent sheets of ice lay across dirty puddles. Horses stretched elegant necks over half-doors, breath rising in moist, gauzy clouds.

Blood, congealed in a hoof print near the shed row corner, signaled something gone wrong.

A Garland County ambulance crew scraped Lester up about the same time the track veterinarian put Sweets down.

Story I heard put out was somehow that mare busted out of her stall during the night, slipped on ice, broke a leg and, in a pain-laced frenzy, stomped Lester to death.

A few workers idly wondered how a homeless bum happened be on row at two in the morning. Several other fellows commented it looked like he'd been beat with a baseball bat, not kicked by a horse.

I heard snatches of talk about an insurance policy Mutts bought on Sweets, which, along with a tote board pay-out and purse, turned a tidy sum.

I got off at midnight and dropped by my round-the-clock diner for breakfast. The place jarred the late shift back to life and rattled morning workers with their hangovers. Dishes and spoons clanged, burnt grease smells hovered above the grill, loud voices argued over weekend ball games, and a nicotine smog tied it all together.

I sat on an end counter stool, ate my usual, and read the morning paper. Finished, I tipped the waitress, got a couple to-go coffees and headed over to the track.

"What's the word, Wilbur?" I handed the gateman a steaming cup.

"Horses already gettin' breezed." He spoke with a distinct drawl.

We stood in silence and sipped the black liquid. Track personnel, up for a couple of hours, moved in quiet silhouettes between stalls and wash stands. An old man raked scattered hay, making soft, scratching noises. Horses stamped against their box walls and snorted gunshots of breath.

"What's Mutt got today?"

"Nuthin'. Done gone." He shook his nappy grey head. "I believes some folks tolt him to move on. You know, without no return ticket."

"What about Lester Groh?"

"They done put him in a pauper grave. Laid that there game little mare out on yonder bone pile."

"Lonely places to rest."

I gazed down track toward weak yellow lights along shed row. Seemed like time balanced, for a moment, somewhere between night uncertainties and morning possibilities. Finally, dark opened his fist and relinquished his hold as dawn lobbed wispy tangerine-pink streaks into the sky. Sparrows twittered and fluttered about, picking up spilled grain. Across the infield, traffic noises swelled as morning rush hour thumped alive.

"Well, who's going to miss a stooper anyway?" I blew on my coffee. "Or another honest mare?"

"Yeah. Who's gonna miss?" He nodded and stared off into the distance with rheumy eyes.

I glanced down at my *Form*, sucked in a deep breath of cold air, and let it out slow. It floated a moment suspended, then vanished.

"Racing starts at one."

About the Author

Nancy Hartney writes about the Deep South of today wrapped in yesterday's clothes. Her roots dig into the piney woods that she rode through on horseback, into the sweat-soaked hardscrabble farms, and into humid passionate nights. Her slice-of-life tales chronicle a time past that is poignant, vivid and sometimes brutal. The reader stares into the eyes of people struggling with living, grasping for understanding, doing the best they know how.

Nancy makes her home in Fayetteville, Arkansas. *Washed in the Water: Tales from the South* is her debut short story collection. Her website is http://nancyhartney.com.

Acknowledgements

〜〜〜〜〜〜〜〜〜〜〜〜〜〜〜〜〜〜〜〜〜

My family and I come from Georgia, and while they have mostly died off or moved further south, I still say I hail from Atlanta. My great-great granddaddy wore grey and fought in *The War*. My daddy was a dirt farmer and Mother a school teacher. Growing up years happened in that strip along the south Georgia-north Florida line on a hardscrabble tobacco farm. We also raised hogs, corn and, for a time, cotton.

Bird shooting and coon hunting marked the fall with tobacco picking, bare feet, and watermelons summer hallmarks. Winter meant busting up pine stumps and hauling oak wood for our fireplace.

Would a collection such as this be complete without casting an eye back on those that struggled with you, against you, and for you? Perhaps yes, perhaps no.

A nod of recognition to my mother whose confidence, values, and love shape me even from her grave. I miss her. My memories curve lovingly around my brother Steve, a bright simpatico life, too soon gone. I must thank my adoptive father whom I have finally forgiven for being himself. He did the best he knew how. A great army of cousins, aunts, uncles, and grandparents marching to different drummers, are remembered for their *joie de vivre* and earthiness. It has taken me a lifetime to embrace the richness of my southern roots and the strength of those in my rural community.

I thank my husband for his tolerance with cluttered rooms when I became obsessed with writing and his patience with reading my work. He is my treasure.

For years, my father-in-law called me "Fancy Nancy." Now he greets me as "the Author." A priceless encouragement.

This project would not have come to fruition without the members of the Northwest Arkansas Writers group. I dare not name them individually but thank them collectively. Sometimes their suggestions caused me anguish; most often they opened new doors. Special gratitude goes to the leaders of that group, author Velda Brotherton and Western writer Dusty Richards, for their positive guidance, spot-on corrections, and constant encouragement.

Thank you is a rather paltry word, even when heartfelt.

Nancy Hartney, 2013

Hartney, Nancy 16551
Washed in the Water
Tales from the South

DATE DUE			